THE FYLDE IN THE 1930s & '40s

by

Catherine Rothwell

Blackpool illuminations, 1949

Dedicated to my sister, Sheila, who shared these years

Published by Hendon Publishing Co. Ltd., Hendon Mill, Nelson, Lancashire.
Text © Catherine Rothwell, 1984
Printed by Fretwell & Brian Ltd., Healey Works, Goulbourne Street, Keighley, West Yorkshire.

Introduction

Television programmes like *The Time of Your Life* have never been so popular, and historical societies continue to proliferate, while their members grow ever more keen to find vintage photographs. Consequently, the years of the thirties and forties are suddenly being focused like a burning glass.

Life as it was lived one hundred years ago is still of interest, but many people are now taking a look at the thirties and forties, because these years lie within their own life span, yet are rapidly slipping into history. At school our children are involved with projects on this period. Maybe young, pertinent questions of 'What was it like?' and a magpie instinct for collecting relevant memorabilia have stimulated their parents' curiosity too. After all, these were amongst the most exciting, tragic, dramatic, exacting decades ever, and if you actually lived through them during the formative years, then, like it or not, you were stamped with indelible impressions.

Local history being essentially an ingredient of national history, it is fitting that the work, thoughts and achievements of everyday people, besides those of the grand and the great, should be set down. Everyday? Ordinary? The thirties and forties produced behaviour and achievement very much out of the ordinary. They called for a type of endurance, courage, faith and character that can take its place beside the best in any century.

As age creeps on, we reach back for the time of our lives most vividly meaningful, knowing that its vitality will one day be replaced by a pervading sense of loss. This pictorial record, enlivened with researched documentation and on-the-spot impressions, may help to save something of the Fylde's contribution towards those stirring twenty years before they drop into oblivion.

It is with gratitude that I acknowledge the providing and sharing of a harvest of pain, passion and fun engendered by marvellous photographs:

The late Mr V Baldwin, the *Blackpool Gazette and Herald*, Mr D. Buckley, Mr J. Burkitt, Mr S. Butterworth, Central Lancashire Archaeological Research Unit, Mr J. Close, Mr B. H. Eardley, Mrs D. Eatough, First Leisure Corporation, Mr F. Greenwood, Mr F. Hearn, Mr. J. Howarth, the *Lancashire Evening Post*, Mr M. Lord, Miss G. H. Marsland, Joyce Morris, Nostalgia Unlimited, Photonia, Mr J. C. Plummer, Mr D. B. Timms, Mr T. Topping, the late Mr A. Turner, Mr F. Williams, Miss D. Winterbotham, the late Mr J. Wright, Mr J. W. Yates, Lancashire Library, Mrs E. Huck, Mr W. Innes.

This photograph from the thirties shows how Blackpool seasiders were bombarded with the sensational and spectacular; here is a small section of what was known as the 'Golden Mile'. At the end of the day money was counted out literally in bucketfuls, and not seaside buckets. If you liked that sort of thing — and it must have lifted the average person out of the ordinary — could there be more concentrated freakishness than Hilda Flack, the giant schoolgirl; Ida Campbell, half-woman; Ubangi savages, and indeed 'the world's greatest freaks in one big show'? Fruit, tripe, oysters, the inevitable sticks of rock, ice-cream and Horlick's malted milk were quickly-available refreshments alongside an impressive tall, brass urn dispensing from morn till night jugs full of tea to take to the sands.

Irish labourers were still migrating to the Fylde at harvest time in the thirties, particularly for potato picking, much to the chagrin of local agricultural workers, who were poorly paid but found themselves undercut by 'Paddy's' acceptance of less. All over the Fylde were still to be found examples of sturdy, three-storeyed houses belonging to well-established yeomen farmers. The top storey extended completely over the length of the building, providing a large dormitory with beds of straw and chaff for these itinerant harvesters. Poulton View Farm at Carleton is a splendid example, still standing.

This typical group from 1932, smoking clay pipes, rough and ready, the butt of many a joke and some malice, would move from farm to farm until the crops were all gathered and it was time to return to Ireland. Cold tea was cheap and refreshing at harvest time. Home-made barley water was considered beneficial and cooling, but this bottle contained whisky on a share and share alike basis, and the rural setting is a far cry from the modern gin palace. March 1932 was, incidentally, the driest month on record since 1908 in the Fylde. As was the custom, on 24th August, traditionally known as Hattock Sunday, farmers and families went out to view the crops from Preesall Hill.

The photograph shows the interior of Cleveleys Hydro with its typically 1930s 'Palm Court' atmosphere. The hydro, once Thornton-Cleveleys' premier hotel, has been replaced by a residential area.

The photograph shows staff on the Knott End platform of the Knott End–Garstang Railway, about 1930. Three little ferry steamers, *Bourne May, Progress* and *Onward* took passengers across the River Wyre. Bourne Arms Hotel, with its fine bowling green, adjoined the railway station and ferry slip. Provided the train, pulled by *Farmer's Friend* or *Knott End* did not break down, the traveller passed Parrox Hall, with its remnants of an old racecourse, Hackensall Hall (once moated, and by the thirties functioning as a farm), Preesall Hill and Charity School, Pilling village and Fluke Hall. Two small platforms and several crossings lay between Nateby and Pilling, and from Nateby to Garstang there was a gradient of only 1 in 73 at the steepest point.

The Garstang and Knott End line extended to Catterall Junction, and considered itself 'one of the most interesting and unique railways in the United Kingdom.' Passenger traffic until 31st March 1930 and the Alkali Works kept going this little railway, and the engine nicknamed the 'Pilling Pig' because of its shrill whistle echoing over the fields. Garstang station's last moments of glory were on the nights of 28th August 1940 and 30th October 1941, when King George VI and Queen Elizabeth slept there in the royal train.

The old goods yard at Lytham seems to sum up the 'death of steam', as it was to be described. Gradually, after the forties, such engines were phased out, but the public did not allow this to happen completely as Lytham's Motive Power Museum helped to prove.

Another photograph from the thirties, of Parkinson's corner shop, which was also Great Carleton post office. Across was the wheelwright's, where Cuthbert and Abigail Harrison once lived with their large family. As William Parkinson opened his post office in 1870 and the family continued to sell groceries and farm produce until a few years before the premises were demolished, it could mean that this was the oldest family-run business in the village. At the far end can be seen Carleton School, where the cane was seldom used. Standing in a corner was punishment enough for most. Sewing, drawing, painting, hockey and cricket were included in the curriculum, and the boys did double trenching in the school garden down Fleetwood Road as a change from 'chalk and talk' from teachers.

Opposite the school was Bowler's, a wooden shop selling Fry's chocolate bars and 'Clixo' toffee. Pomfret cakes and penny bottles of ginger beer, dandelion-and-burdock, lemonade and cream soda were delights to look forward to when school was over in those halcyon days.

In 1949 the name of a Fylde man, Albert Heggett, went round the world when it was revealed that his pet dog boiled his kettle every morning. Albert, named after the Prince-Consort, was born on the Sandringham estate, and recalled Queen Victoria visiting his cottage — 'a very homely person.' A Fleetwood labrador, Toby, belonging to Norman Grisenthwaite, not only saved a house from being burned down, but stood over a live hand-grenade on the beach, keeping children away until the arrival of the police. January 1949 saw the Fylde plunged into grief with the news, on 7th January, of the feared loss of the *Goth* with all hands. Owned by the Wyre Steam Trawling Company and managed by Merchants Ltd., she came from Hull in 1946. The average age of the crew was twenty-nine, one of whom, deck-hand Parker, awarded the D.S.M. for bravery when his minesweeper was attacked by a German plane in 1942, had been married only a fortnight before.

Norman Grisenthwaite, who was on the *Goth,* had survived the wrecking of *Nordale* off the Mull of Kintyre in 1940. On that occasion he was hauled up a 600-foot cliff. He also survived being washed overboard from the *Flying Admiral*. Such were the hazards of steam trawling. Norman's labrador pined with grief at his loss. Fishermen's families suffered agony. The calm of steam trawlers moored in glassy water in Wyre Dock, Fleetwood, tells only one side of the story.

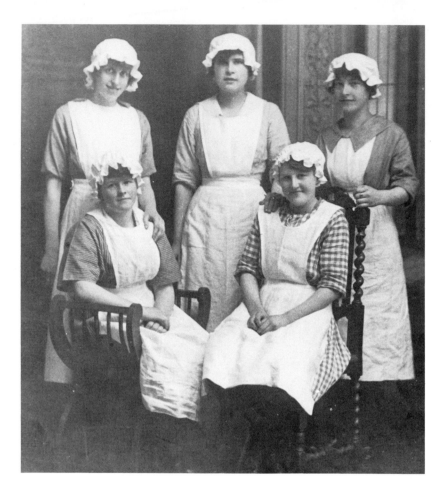

The horse was still important in 1930. Processions and parades featured decorated horses, bicycles, children dressed to the nines and brass bands. Dobbin or Dapple would work a milk or coal round during the day with his tail plaited, and be borrowed for use at funerals or weddings next day, tail let down, brushed and almost touching the ground. Black horses were favoured for funerals.

Milk was delivered in brightly-shone kits, with a tap at the bottom to measure a gill, pint or quart into jugs which customers brought to the float. It poured forth creamy and frothy, still warm from the cow. The kits were carefully rinsed and scalded, otherwise the milk would have gone sour; fresh, sieved and cooled, it would keep for up to a week. Cleanliness was such that yard walls were scrubbed so that washing hanging on the line would not soil. Wages were about a pound a week. As there was as yet little motor traffic, games were still played in the street: bobs and checks, shuttlecock and battledore, diabolo, top and whip, marbles, conkers, hopscotch, skipping and nuts-in-May. With half a yard of old lace curtain and paper roses on a ribbon-bound hoop, you had the makings of a May Queen set to sing round the village houses and farms in hopes of collecting a few pennies. These were spent on mineral water bottles fitted with marble stoppers (cod bottles, now collectors' pieces). A way of life that had persisted for centuries, by the early years of the thirties was virtually dead.

Farms like this (Bonny's at Revoe in 1932) began to disappear. Centuries-old cobbles in yards and barns stubbornly resisted the bulldozers. Five-barred farm gates rusted off their hinges, and much of the land was taken for council house estates all over the Fylde.

This group of five includes Edie and Maggie Cardwell of Carleton. All the girls worked at Parkhurst bakery, Blackpool, which was one of a number kept busy supplying the needs of visitors to the Fylde. By the thirties, girls who had hitherto worked only on the farms or at home were finding jobs in Blackpool, which grew in popularity as a resort year by year. In childhood, Edie and Maggie were content with a Sunday School trip to Lytham each year in a charabanc, and the Shrove Tuesday tea party. Their mother baked all the bread for the family, and like many others was up all night making paper roses for the archway at Castle Gardens when the crowning of the Rose Queen came round.

Possibly the greatest excitement that ever occurred in Carleton was the occasion in May 1931 when Abigail Whalley, a rich widow living in Robin's Lane, was found murdered. Twenty detectives concentrated on the area for over forty-eight hours, sifting every available clue and having no sleep. The Chief Constable of Lancashire, W. Trubshaw, appealed to the public to come forward. '. . . the clue of the lavender seller caused some sensation.' It remains, however, to this day, an unsolved crime.

It took many years' hard work to bring this 'Free Pier' into being, but as the 1936 photograph shows, it was all worthwhile, proving a popular draw to holiday crowds in the Fylde and a delightful social rendezvous all year round for the town of Fleetwood, until a disastrous fire destroyed it. 'The cinema over the sea, showing the world's best productions . . . magnificent Deck Café, spacious amusements arcade, Vita Glass Lounge, Belisha Parade, accommodation for 3,000, Pierfect entertainment, Pierfect surroundings, Pierfect looking . . .' Need one say more? The happy crowds on this perfect June day, with Union Jacks fluttering proudly, could visualize neither a mass of twisted girders in the years hence, nor the Second World War only three years away.

Fylde man Fred Woods, son of Tom Woods the printer who was involved in the first edition of Porter's *History of the Fylde,* rose to some importance. Always an inventive person, he was as a young man one of the few people in the country interested in sustained flight without power, contributing his experiences to the magazines *Flight* and *Aero.* For practice his 30-foot sections of aeroplane were taken over to Preesall, ferried on two punts fitted with floats. He became development engineer to Marconi Marine for merchant ships and to the Marconi Wireless Company for naval work. In 1930 he was tackling the problem of direction finders for trawlers. Although Fylde born-and-bred, whilst working for Marconi he was chosen as Mayor of Chelmsford twice, and had the honour to entertain the first reigning sovereign to visit Chelmsford since the first Queen Elizabeth. A friend of Mr Norman St. John Stevas, he was honoured by the commissioning of a commemorative bronze in his likeness. The photograph shows Fred assembling one of his prototype machines in the cobbled yard in Fleetwood where his uncle's sail-making loft was situated.

Next to J. W. Harrison's grocery shop, which sold Robinson's bread and St. Bruno tobacco (according to enamelled signs on the wall) was Carleton Motor Works (Tel. Poulton 114) 'with a fleet of Daimler cars available for all purposes . . . weddings, tours, funerals.' The proprietor, J. Marshall, supplied Pratt's commercial motor spirit. It is thought that the three men in the photograph are Joe Marshall, Frank Pilling and Harry Humphreys. Diagonally opposite lay competition in the shape of Carleton Garage, where Fylde Ford now stands.

When this photograph was taken near Castle Gardens, Carleton, the internal combustion engine was bringing about a revolution. These cross roads, once Town End, where maypole dancing was practised, street games played and the hurdy-gurdy man accompanied by his monkey had churned out delightful tunes, by the thirties were transformed. Carleton had hitherto been typical of a Fylde community, spread round a 'four-lane-ends', with its green, well, inn and school. Its maypole was hewn out by the joiner, who had his shop on the site of the present butcher's on Blackpool Road corner. Sparrows were trapped in cinder riddles propped up with sticks over corn, later to be skinned and put into pies. The advent of the motor car, motor bike and 'charries' turned thoughts in other directions.

Poulton Road, looking towards Poulton from Castle Gardens, Carleton, is pictured in the early 1930s. Carefree walking on roads devoid of traffic was possible. Across from the group of girls is the blacksmith's shop, alongside old Kilshaw's Farm. Behind the girl in the white pinafore can be seen Nellie Parkinson's shop, originally thatched and lime-washed. Nellie sold vegetables, paraffin oil (which stood next to the flour bin), loose butter, lard, treacle and a grand variety of boiled sweets at two ounces for one penny. The fishman called at the village on Tuesdays and Fridays, and Charlie Butler, butcher, came round with his cart on other days. Donkey stones, from Parkinson's, were used to clean doorsteps. In return for rags, the rag and bone man gave cream and blue stones for sprucing up the flags in front of dwellings Even in the thirties many streets were 'unadopted', and those who had flagstones were very proud. Kitchen stoves were cleaned with blacklead polish and emery paper. The old cottages alongside the girls are still there, but Nellie's shop has been pulled down. Behind, in the orchard, the Parkinsons kept cows, making milk available twice a day. Apples, plums, William pears and hazelnuts in season were obtainable from this orchard, and the good life was further enhanced by grapes grown at Carleton's Orchard Farm, which supplied Fleetwood market.

On an October morning in 1932 the trawler *Margaret Rose* steamed through the lock pits, loaded to her scupper doors with 340 tons of coal, 90 tons of rice and 2 tons of salt. This was no ordinary trip for the pride of the Boston Deep Sea Fisheries fleet. The 144-foot vessel was off to explore for hake under the command of Skipper Walter Holmes, because the fish for which Fleetwood was famed, and which had made her the premier hake port in the country, had become scarce. New fishing grounds therefore had to be found. It meant steaming hundreds of miles butting through gales, and losing one catch so tremendous it could not be hauled in — 'everything started parting and we lost the lot'. This haul, however, was not hake, but fine quality haddock. Although the experiment failed as far as the discovering of hake grounds was concerned, the *Margaret Rose* made history on this voyage by working areas no British vessel had touched before. Shortly afterwards she was transferred to Pêcheries de la Marine, a French company, and rechristened the *Marguerite Rose*. From Boulogne, Skipper Holmes pioneered Norwegian deep-water fishing, landing excellent catches.

The group in front of Fleetwood's grain elevator represent a deputation from Newfoundland, one of many attempts made during the thirties and forties to stimulate trade and rationalize prices in the industry. The fight goes on.

On Easter Monday, 21st April 1930, Lytham had a big event when Mrs J. T. Clifton opened its new cinema, which presented the 'talkie' picture *Gold Diggers of Broadway*. The Blackpool Tower Company had acquired from the representatives of Talbot Clifton 1,116 square yards of land in Clifton Street and South Clifton Street on 8th August 1928. Two dwelling houses and shops, known as Wykeham Cottages (later demolished) together with the site cost £5,572 16s 4d, but total expenditure by 31st October 1934 had amounted to £42,926 4s 5d.

The Lytham Estate Office undertook not to grant any other lease for the erection of a cinema for five years within a radius of three miles of Clifton Square, Lytham, excluding St. Annes and the sites of Lytham Pier and Pavilion, the old sites intended for a picture house in Pleasant Street.

By December 1930 the company was negotiating for the Art Picture House, Fleetwood, where Western Electric sound equipment had been installed. The talkies may have been all the rage, but sedate Lytham preserved its leafy, older-world image, as shown in this photograph of Lytham Market Hall. In September 1956 this building was purchased by Messrs William and Bernard Blackhurst.

One stormy Fylde night the stern voice of David Leadbetter, coxswain of the Fleetwood lifeboat, could be heard above the pounding waves and the two maroons fired: "It's nooan a dog. It's a lad. It's that Percy Mather. If there's owt exciting going on, he's sure to be in't midst of it. Turn him out.' From under the thwarts a boy was hauled and dropped on to the floor of the lifeboat house. But young Percy would not take that answer. He ran like a hare to North End, where the tug was getting up steam to tow out the lifeboat to the wreck, and under cover of darkness crept aboard. There were halfway down the estuary before he was discovered again, busying himself as a crew member.

One of the Fylde's greatest sons and Methodists, Percy was fascinated by the sea, and years later, from Indo-China, immersed in missionary work, he wrote with nostalgic love of the Fleetwood ferry-boat. He found time to compile a Mongolian dictionary. When he came home on first furlough to the Esplanade family house, he had not seen a white woman for sixteen years. *Chronicle* reporter Mr Roberts got the scoop of his lifetime talking to Percy as a friend, for he would meet none of the horde of other reporters, having come home solely to recruit six other young men for the China Inland Mission.

The photograph shows Percy Mather in Chinese dress. Unremitting hard work, and disease transmitted by appalling conditions, led to the early death of this unselfish Christian gentleman.

In the early thirties adverse weather affected Fylde fish sales. On New Year's Eve 1930 there were gales of up to 70 m.p.h. Sea passages from Liverpool took ten hours. Two trawlers reported losses of their small boats during the gales, and a British Legion Club was struck by lightning in September of that year. High tides and winds moved a large concrete block from the sea defences in August 1931, and the following year the Fylde (throughout its history buffeted by the elements) had very rough seas in April. The *River Kent* lost her rudder during a gale and was all day at the mercy of wind and weather. J. Marr & Sons' *Jacinta* drifted for hours in a 70 m.p.h. gale in October 1932. A blizzard in March 1933 smashed the woodwork and ripped the sails of trawler *Gypsy Queen*; several vehicles and buildings were struck by lightning. Gales and heavy seas wreaked hundreds of pounds' worth of damage to the Isle of Man boats in August 1933. Fog, high tides, gales and rough seas characterized Fylde weather in the early months of 1934, but mercifully July brought a heat-wave which 'made a lot of money'.

This excellent photograph is of the Isle of Man steamer *Mona's Isle* leaving Fleetwood in the settled weather of that month.

This photograph shows the building of Blackpool's Derby Baths in 1938. Although the main block was completed before the war, it was never officially opened. The ceremony should have been performed by Lord Derby, but it had to be postponed because of the war. Not until 10th November 1965 were there 'two openings in one'. This time the ceremony was performed by Lord Derby, grandson of the previous one mentioned. The splendour and Olympic proportions of the main block are mirrored by this account of the official opening with details of a new remedial section: '. . . five marble shampoo and massage slabs; Scottish and Vichy douches, with hot or cold, fresh or sea water; two vapour rooms; three Turkish rooms; three bathrooms for hot, fresh and sea water baths; pine and hydropathic treatments; gymnasium etc.' In true Blackpool tradition, grand style rather than half-hearted approach was the aim.

February 1930 saw the start of a £29,000 project on new sea defences, but a great battering by the ocean opened up a fissure several hundred yards long in October 1935. Building inspector Major Ernest Todd, with Mr Thomas Parkinson Gerrard from the Surveyor's Department at Fleetwood, inspected the damage. Urgently, fleets of lorries, end to end, carried tons of rubblestone day after day to fill up the breach and create a specially reinforced apron. Many times since then the wall has had to be repaired. This photograph shows an occasion when the inrushing tide trapped a Rapier 19 crane involved in repairing the sea defences at Rossall.

An article written in May 1933 refers to this beautiful building, Lytham Hall, as 'a sad house' because it remained shuttered and empty much of the time, its owner, the turbulent Squire John Talbot Clifton, being in distant lands. The Cliftons went back in direct unbroken male line to 1060, King William Rufus having bestowed on a Clifton knight ten carucates of land in the Fylde. Wanderlust pursued Talbot Clifton up to his death: Africa, Greenland, Sudan, Siberia, Peru, San Francisco, Canada, Alaska; and in his major travels he was always alone. He found, in voluntary exile, 'that peace which civilisation and its currency do not hold for me.' This restless Viking of a man, who met his wife Violet, a woman of apparently matching mettle and spirit, in the Andes, found it impossible to settle down to life in Lytham Park, supervising tenants and land. After being given the freedom of Lytham St. Annes he no-longer lived there at all, but bought Kildalton Castle on the Hebridean Isle of Islay.

His last objective was to cross the desert from the Niger to Timbuktu, but he suffered a seizure and died at Dakar, aged sixty. The coffin, brought from Tenerife to London on a small Norwegian vessel, was lashed to the taffrail on the boatdeck, open to wind and sea spume. A man of magnificent stature, known to some famous people in the early years of this century, Talbot Clifton may possibly be the model for one of the characters of Evelyn Waugh's *Brideshead Revisited*.

The lifeboat *Maud Pickup* sailed out of Fylde history in the year 1930. Operating since 1894, gift of James Pickup of Southport, she had the most distinguished career of any lifeboat on the Fylde coast, saving 117 lives. In 1930 the station at Fleetwood was temporarily closed down, but such protest was made that in 1933 it reopened with a new boat, *Sir Fitzroy Clayton*, provided by the Lifeboat Institution at a cost of £3,081.

The photograph of *Sir Fitzroy Clayton* features from the left: Revd Clarkson; Mr William Ball (Hon. Secretary); Deaconess Anna; Mrs R. Knowles; the Hon. Secretary of the Ladies' Lifeboat Guild; Mrs J. Wood; Alderman G. M. Robinson (the Mayor); Mr W. Hodkinson; Mrs J. W. Dandy (President, Ladies' Lifeboat Guild); Mr J. Wood (Branch President); Jeff Wright (coxswain); Miss Ann Elvidge (Fleetwood Fishing Queen); Councillor H. Rawcliffe; John Leadbetter; Louis Eastwood; Sid Hill (mechanic); H. Wright; R. Bright; Jim Leadbetter. The setting is the old Fleetwood Lifeboat House.

This lifeboat functioned until 1935, saving four lives, to be followed by *Frederick H. Pilley,* which operated until the year the Second World War broke out. *Ann Letitia Russell,* which came on the scene in 1939, was of a very different design from *Maud Pickup,* with her sails and oars. Built of Honduras mahogany, 41ft. 6in. long, double-skinned with an oilskin lining between the two thicknesses, *Ann Letitia* had eight watertight compartments and a watertight engine room. In the event of being swamped, she could empty herself of water in eleven seconds, and should she capsize, the bottom was fitted with handrails. She could carry 75 people in rough weather. Only the mechanic was a full-time employee, but the crew received 15s for the first two hours and 4s an hour afterwards in summer, £1 and 5s in winter. One of the most hazardous trips was made in 1935 to help the trawler *Sarba*.

Open yards between the old Blackpool Corporation stables were roofed over to provide spacious areas for the Illuminations Department's artists and electricians, and work is in progress on an Illuminations tableau at Rigby Road sheds in 1938, with no thought of a blackout the following year. The world-famed Blackpool Illuminations, still visited from far and wide, were inaugurated in 1897 with five trams lit by batteries, providing glowing loyal slogans to mark Queen Victoria's Diamond Jubilee. By 1930 electricity for the venture, which had grown in leaps and bounds, was supplied almost entirely by Penwortham Power Station, one of the first enterprises linked with the National Grid scheme. That year, large illuminated tableaux featured on Bispham Cliffs. Originally part of the Electricity and Tramway Departments under Charles Furness, as the 'lights' grew in popularity a separate entity had to be created in January 1936. Sir Josiah Stamp, Chairman of the L.M.S. Railway Company, switched on the illuminations by remote control. (The railways brought 900,000 passengers to the town in 1,750 trains). The coming of war hurried staff to build air raid shelters, and there were no more lights until 1949.

This peaceful, sylvan view of the church and graveyard of St. Chad, Poulton-le-Fylde, in 1934 does not mirror the fierce controversy that had arisen that year over the living. Originally owned by the Fleetwood-Hesketh family, the living of the church was still in private hands when an attempt was made to sell it. News leaked out in the village, leading to an uproar because it should first have been offered to the parish. Seven hundred pounds had to be raised in less than three months, a lot of money in the sparse thirties, but, led by Councillor Haythornthwaite, a group did achieve this figure and the living became the property of the parish in 1931.

An exciting find in the tower not long after was a collection of eighteenth-century books, well wrapped, which proved to be a library of eighty bound volumes, one of a number endowed up and down the country by Thomas Bray for the use of the clergy. Doctor Bray was connected with the S.P.C.K., 1979 being his 250th anniversary, which was celebrated in London and attended by the Queen. The Vicar of Poulton and his wife were invited on account of the town's complete Bray Library. The precious volumes are now kept for better preservation at John Rylands Library, Manchester, on permanent loan. Mr. Baldwin's photograph has also weathered the years well, and shows the different appearance of the churchyard in the 1930s compared with today.

The gardens of Claughton Hall, near Brock, were open to the public on 11th August 1937, and many visitors came to satisfy their curiosity, for these gardens and heronry were at one time much talked about. The conservatories produced splendid grapes; a hailstorm was reputed to have smashed 8,000 squares of glass and strewn bunches of grapes, torn from the vines by the violence of the storm. Amateur florists and gardeners were interested in one part of the gardens adjacent to the house where an American Aloe was flowering. At one time it was thought that this plant did not flower until it was one hundred years old, and then only once. The American Aloe in Claughton Hall Gardens was about seventy years old when it flowered, with leaves 15 feet in length and 14 inches wide. The 'old squire', Mr Brockholes, was interested in fattening Highland cattle, which were sent to Preston butchers' shops for show at Christmas. He insisted when the railway passed through his estates on the building of a handsome bridge with the crest of the Brockholes family, a badger, in the stonework. At Claughton Hall are also fish ponds. In the last century an interesting find was made in the park, consisting of an urn of baked clay containing weapons, ornaments and bones, possibly those of a Viking buried within the tumulus.

The gardener is tending two unusual graves at Great Singleton, one of a horse, the other of dogs. Over the model village reigned Mr T. H. Miller, lord of the manor, who owned a famous shire stallion, Honest Tom, which won many prizes in shows. At its death, the animal's head was preserved for posterity, for many years being kept at Mowbreck Hall, where the Lancashire Agricultural Show was held. The tombstone of Honest Tim in Singleton Park has carved upon it:

> Great Honest Tom lies here at rest
> After a life of fame,
> The laurels o'er his grave attest
> He earned a champion's name.

The photograph, thought to date from 1948, reveals, alongside, a second stone, dedicated 'To the memory of all our faithful dogs', erected by the squire in 1905.

Not far from the parish church of Lytham, embedded in the hedge of the cricket field, the observant visitor, years ago, would notice the socket of a stone cross, said to mark one of the resting places of the body of St. Cuthbert when being carried to Durham. Sir Cuthbert Clifton, the first squire of Lytham, built his house in the seventeenth century on the site of the ruins of St. Cuthbert's Priory, which was entirely destroyed after the dissolution of the monasteries. The photograph shows the occasion when a commemorative service was held in front of a new cross placed in the old socket. The sanctification of the new cross in the old socket was witnessed by a crowd which again clearly shows the fashions then prevalent, even a 'sit up and beg' bicycle. The cross's decline is poignantly reflected in the march of history, from the days of 1188, when the Benedictine priory flourished, to comparatively modern times. Ancient documents tell of the priors' hospitality, the keeping up of customs, 'gifts to the minstralles and beggars', the boy bishop's feast and the payment of Peter's pence. The Revd Canon Hawkins was instrumental in having the ruined wayside cross near Lowther Gardens replaced.

On 15th September 1934 the freedom of the Borough of Blackpool was presented to the Rt. Hon. the Earl of Derby, K.G., in the Tower Ballroom, Blackpool. The photograph shows the guests of honour at the high table during the dinner organized to celebrate the occasion. Lord Derby is the moustached gentleman wearing the star under his row of medals. Next but one to his left is Lord Stanley, his son. The family, extensive landowners in the Fylde, were generous with their time and money, always willing to attend functions and enterprises benefiting the area. Lord Derby's growing corpulence in later years caused some difficulty, one such occasion being when he had to climb up to a lifeboat made ready for launching, but he passed all off with a smile and a joke, and must have been the most familiar figure up and down Lancashire in the thirties.

This photograph, dated August 1948, is unmistakeable. Field Marshal Lord Montgomery is receiving the freedom of Blackpool Borough in the Town Hall, Blackpool. Together with Winston Churchill, who was here, there, and everywhere, likewise receiving the freedom of cities and being decked with honours after the conclusion of the Second World War, 'Monty' must have had the most famous face in the world. 'Desert Rats' from the Fylde who served in the Eighth Army at El Alamein talk of his suddenly appearing beside them in battle. Mingling with his troops was inspiration and recipe for victory.

A photograph from the mid 1930s of Broadwater Crossing, Fleetwood, again reveals the scarcity of motor-car traffic. The lamp standard of wrought iron, printed newspaper posters and enamelled advertising signs have since been replaced by their modern counterparts or merely dispensed with. The tram track still crosses the road at this point and the model of the tram is interesting. Blackpool Transport Department stressed the common interest shared by Fleetwood and Blackpool in street transport during 1933.

. . . Fleetwood supplies the electric current for the propulsion of cars . . . and Blackpool provides the cars . . . before the end of 1933 it is expected that a fleet of luxury cars will be in use daily and the two towns will then be only thirty minutes apart. The new cars will be speedy, safe, comfortable, well-lighted and heated and will give really good travel so that no matter how good or bad the weather may be, the journey between the two towns will be done in absolute comfort.

Riley & Sons milliner's and outfitter's shop in Corporation Street, Blackpool, was pulled down in 1936, the year of Blackpool's Jubilee celebrations, commemorating sixty years of incorporation. That year there was a great fire, when the municipal offices and Messrs Boots in Corporation Street were burned down on 7th October. A fireman was killed. Riley's had to sell off all stocks after being in business over sixty-five years. Drapers' shops in the Fylde did very well and generally were long-established. Another example was A. J. Priestley & Son Ltd. of Fleetwood, whose roots went back nearly one hundred years, for there was an unbroken link between the small draper's shop started in 1863 next to the Fielden Library, in Dock Street, and the modern shop on Lord Street. The Priestley business was formed into a limited company in 1941, and when Mr Priestley, a former Chamber of Trade president, died in 1944, his son, Mr C. J. Priestley, became managing director.

Brine wells at Preesall, photographed in 1932. By 1934 the salt works were almost demolished. They were referred to in the *Penny Guide to Knott End and Garstang . . . Unique towns in the Fylde and Over Wyre district,* as 'the establishments denoted by field shafts similar in construction to colliery headings. These are brine pumping stations in connection with Preesall Salt Mines, an industry carried on by the United Alkali Company who have extensive works at Thornton on the opposite side of the river Wyre.' The rock salt mined, of a sparkling, white, flocculent nature, in demand as far away as India, was shipped from a nearby jetty. The mining, however, caused alarming subsidence in the area and it had to cease.

From the rock salt to rock — this photograph dated 1938 shows Fylde seaside rock makers in their factory. A year later women were working in munitions factories or in furniture making, becoming skilled French polishers. Machines for compressing waste paper into bales were obtained by Fylde towns, and every item that could be recycled was put to use.

Ten years after the laying of the foundation stone of the £30,000 promenade at Thornton-Cleveleys, Lord Stanley attended the official opening of Jubilee Gardens, which occurred in Coronation year, on 1st May 1937. The gardens with all their facilities made an ideal setting for the happy celebration. Children's vouchers were issued free for amusements — train rides, pitch-and-putt, paddling and tennis. Thornton-Cleveleys brass band played. Tea for senior citizens (although they were not so described in those days) was served at the Royal Hotel, and inevitably a procession was organized.

The photograph shows Lord Stanley bowling the first wood on the new green at Jubilee Gardens, Thornton-Cleveleys, after unveiling the commemoration stone and cutting the tape. Coronation Year itself was a busy time for queens. Miss Vera Greenwood, Cotton Queen of Britain, visited Thornton-Cleveleys in July 1937. She attended functions with the Fishing Queen of Fleetwood.

Rather more important is the occasion of the visit to the Fylde in 1938 of King George VI and Queen Elizabeth, now the Queen Mother. The postman on the extreme right adds both a homely touch and a reminder of G.P.O. uniform and delivery, thirties vintage, as he waits patiently at the Marine Gardens, Fleetwood.

On April 5th 1931 Kubelik, the world-famous violinist, appeared at the Opera House, Winter Gardens, Blackpool. Hannen Swaffer spoke there on Spiritualism on 22nd November, and Stanley Baldwin made a political appearance in 1932. The photograph depicts a gala occasion, with Sandy Powell probably voicing his once-famed question 'Can you hear me mother?', a somewhat different call from that of the divine Adelina Patti. She appeared on 20th August 1900 in the 'Greatest Concert of the Century'. Under the same roof were the Empress Ballroom, with its marvellous parquet floor laid on 2,000 spiral springs, and the Indian Lounge, together 'the most sumptuous and palatial hall in the world'. It was always difficult to go one better than Blackpool.

A Kirkham backyard of the late thirties; it could be one of hundreds in the 'cottonopolis' mill town. Where does mother begin to tidy up all this 'hugger-mugger', with Spot considering walking the plank, and Dad having hung up his clogs? Clogs were essential for old and young alike, and were not dying out until Old Father Time nudged the forties. In all Fylde the best-known cloggers for generations were the Clegg family, with businesses in Kirkham, Poulton, Fleetwood and Thornton. They later stocked boots and shoes when families had more income and were considering the wearing of clogs 'beneath them' and rather 'common'. Little girls' mothers boasted that their daugthers had never worn them, and some small boys ate their hearts out because they were not allowed to. However, in the early thirties there were Fylde families so poor that they had no footwear at all. Only on the docks did the wearing of clogs persist. Safe, warm, hard-wearing footgear for the lumpers and merchants, it is still traditional.

There is no doubt that true clog-making was a craft to be proud of, for the materials were all prepared by hand; even the seasoning and shaping of the wooden soles was hand-done. Fleetwood Museum possesses the last pair of hand-made clogs produced in the town by Lewis Albon, who served his time to it and could read your character from your feet, or rather, from how your gait shaped your clogs.

Mr Richard Spencer, M.B.E., the author of *Reminiscences of Freckleton*, pinpoints 23rd August 1944 as the darkest day in the history of this Fylde village, with its records going back to Norman times. The postcard shows the centre of the village of Freckleton.

At the Church of England School, term had begun only the day before. Hot weather suddenly veered to sultry, storm conditions. Heralded by a loud crack, out of the sky an American test flight plane hurtled down on to Alan Whittle's snack bar opposite the school, killing all those inside, staff and people sheltering. The plane's impetus carried it into the Infants' department of the school, where thirty-eight children and two teachers met their death. This appalling tragedy, reminiscent of Aberfan some twenty years later, led to a mass funeral for the children at the parish church and separate funerals for other victims throughout the following week. The Americans tended children who were wounded at their hospital on Warton Station and flew Bing Crosby out from America to sing to them. Following this plane disaster the new Church of England School was opened in School Lane.

Outside St. Thomas's Church, Garstang, in February, 1940, townspeople gaze in amazement at the depth of frozen snow. It was one of the most phenomenal winters of the century and made the first year of the Second World War even harder to bear. Railway engines and motor cars were buried for months. Snow fell until it touched the eaves of houses after drifting in some areas. Cattle and sheep were lost and transport made impossible, dangerous or very difficult. Some villages were cut off entirely, and food supplies had to be dropped for beasts and men in Bleasdale.

Fortunately, although the air raid sirens sounded many times, the Fylde suffered little from enemy action. To help repel any invasion by sea, posts were set in fields and barbed wire entanglements laid on the shore at Blackpool, Lytham St. Annes and Fleetwood. In July 1940 German planes dropped a string of incendiary bombs near Freckleton, followed by a 'screaming' bomb whose unearthly, previously unheard sound rattled the air raid wardens on duty at Warton A.R.P. post. One Sunday night in September 1940 the droning of enemy bombers accompanied a string of 110-lb bombs dropping on Warton and Freckleton, demolishing a smithy, but not the blacksmith's house, where that day a large quantity of jam had been made. Story has it that Lord Haw-haw, traitor and chief announcer on the German foreign service, reported a successful raid on a jam factory at Freckleton.

The worst bombing occurred on the night of 12th March 1941 at 10.45 p.m., when two land mines dropped on Warton, smashing thousands of panes of glass in Harbour Lane, Church Road and Bryning near the Birley Arms Hotel. Sudden exposure to frosty air killed plants, and it took weeks to replace the glass. The craters were almost big enough to swallow a house. In April 1941 a German plane was shot down, falling in the mud flats of the Ribble, leaving one survivor who was cared for at Lytham Hospital prior to being sent to a P.O.W. camp.

These ladies of the W.V.S. canteen for His Majesty's Forces, Weeton, did sterling war work in the area at that time.

On the dot of 11.15 a.m. on 3rd September 1939 came the voice of Neville Chamberlain from 10 Downing Street: 'I have to tell you . . . this country is at war with Germany.' Tremendous preparations had to be made in the context of a state of unpreparedness. The Air Raid Precautions Act caused food committees to be formed, air raid sirens to be installed, buildings sandbagged, and barrage balloons to rise. Decontamination squads were formed, for there was a genuine fear of the use of poison gas. Thirty-eight million gas masks had been distributed since the Munich crisis of the previous year. 'Dad's Army', the Local Defence Volunteers, practised zealously, using wooden dummy rifles until the real thing arrived.

Over 40,000 evacuees were ordered to Fleetwood alone, from the inland cities, as the Fylde was considered a safe area, 1,600 arriving in September 1939.

The photograph shows practice on the cliffs at Bispham — simulated action during an air raid. The second photograph, February 1941, graphically presents the first Fylde all-ladies' stirrup-pump team practising in Fleetwood's Pharos Street. Next to tin hats, pixie hoods were favourite civilian female wartime head gear.

H. M. S. FLEETWOOD.

The wreck of the Faroese schooner *Stella Marie* close to the Wyre Light was probably the last remnant of the romantic days of sail seen on the Fylde coast. It occurred in 1941 when she was carrying a cargo of fish to Wyre Dock, Fleetwood. A gale was blowing and a heavy, dangerous sea pounded the shores, but Jeff Wright, coxswain, managed to get alongside with his crew. Seven of the eight men aboard the schooner jumped into the water and were pulled aboard, avoiding by seconds being crushed against the wreck. Almost immediately an enormous sea turned the lifeboat right round. The steel pintle of the rudder buckled and jammed, making it very difficult to get back, but having picked up the skipper of the schooner, they made it into Fleetwood.

In May 1937 Fleetwood, which gave its name to the sloop H.M.S. *Fleetwood,* provided a fitting week of recognition during the latter's visit. Each day the ship was inspected by an average of 8,000 people. During their stay, officers and men were given the freedom of the town, cementing the bond of friendship. As the ship approached, large crowds enthusiastically waved hats and handkerchiefs; greetings were signalled from the Mount.

Commander A. C. Chapman, with his officers, received a civic welcome at the Town Hall. Every day was full: Monday, civic welcome; Tuesday, dinner given by the Fleetwood Fishing Vessel Owners' Association, who presented a handsome silver cup; Wednesday, corporation dinner; Thursday, 'at home' on the ship. On Friday it was the crew's turn; they were guests in the Marine Hall. Wednesday coincided with Queen Mary's bithday, when H.M.S. *Fleetwood* fired a royal salute of twenty-one guns. Fleetwood Grammar School children lined up alongside. Fortunately the size of the ship enabled her to moor at the quay. The town clerk, Mr J. Bell; the Mayor, Alderman W. E. Simpson; and the Deputy Mayor, Alderman Charles Saer, were busy officials.

Dr Edith Summmerskill, M.P., Parliamentary Secretary to the Ministry of Food, was another eminent visitor to the Fylde (May 1947). She made a tour of Wyre Dock, where she was presented with a prime haddock. Those were the days of Icelandic fishing, and the week of Dr Summerskill's visit coincided with the arrival of the British-built Icelandic trawler *Ingolfur Arnarnason,* one of the most up-to-date fishing vessels in the world. One of four ultra-modern vessels provided for the people of Reykjavik by the newly-formed Icelandic government, it landed 45,000 stone of fish and made £13,900. Three of the crew had brought their wives who, in spite of sea-sickness on the way, quickly prepared for a shopping expedition in Blackpool. Edith Summerskill was told of important problems soon to be discussed in London on 23rd May 1947 — the employment of Poles in British trawlers to relieve the crew shortage then prevailing, and the securing of 100 per cent trade unionism in the industry.

The photograph shows Dr Summerskill signing the visitors' book at Fleetwood Town Hall. She received her haddock in that part of the dock where the fish auctions were held.

In 1941 Blackpool adopted the cruiser H.M.S. *Penelope,* which was sunk three years later by an enemy submarine. Warship Week, 1941, saw National Savings Campaigns held all over the country and Blackpool people provided £1,504,349 towards the purchase of H.M.S. *Penelope.* The crew were continuously supplied from the town with cigarettes, food and clothing. These historic links are still maintained with the present *Penelope,* a Leander class frigate of 3,000 tons launched in 1963.

Ian Palmer had particular memories of the sinking of the cruiser in the Mediterranean in 1944, for he was reported missing, presumed dead, and honoured with a funeral service. 'We were heading for Anzio when a U-boat torpedo hit the engine room, a second struck us and we had no hope. Crew abandoned ship, which sank in seconds with a loss of 370. There were 178 survivors.' But Ian was rescued by an American boat, and after being demobbed came back on a thank-you visit with others saved from the sea. Eventually he was to set up a business in the town.

The photograph shows the welcoming of Captain A. D. Nicholl, Commander, who remained wounded at his post on the bridge of H.M.S. *Penelope.* Captain Nicholl inspected the sea cadets forming a guard of honour on 11th July 1942 in front of the Town Hall, Blackpool.

The modern growth of the Fylde is nowhere more dramatically expressed than in the growth of Poulton-le-Fylde. Under the 1931 census the latter's population was 3,366. In 1934 the boundaries of the Urban District were extended and the pre-war population estimated at 6,000. By the end of the forties this figure was 7,278 and it has continued to rise ever since. The area, extended on 1st April 1934, increased the Urban District by 707 acres from the parish of Carleton, and 776 acres from the parish of Hardhorn-with-Newton, a total of 2,410 acres.

Samuel Frederick Stansfield of Oaklands, Poulton, died on 3rd April 1932, aged 63, his wife Jeannie ('Queenie') on 16th January 1939. They hailed from Rawtenstall but loved Poulton, which took them to its heart for their generosity and homeliness. Tragedy struck in 1923 when they lost their only child Jean. In Moorland Road Cemetery is a beautiful memorial, a carved, white marble angel, but the Jean Stansfield Memorial Park built on Glebe land alongside the old Vicarage Lane is the memorial given to the town in her name.

The Stansfields were examples of many hundreds who migrated to the old-world market town. In this photograph of the late 1940s the centre building functioned alone as the Town Hall. A much larger post office had to be built and the old property to the left demolished.

To the east of Garstang on top of a small hill, the scanty remains of one of the few castles in the county (perhaps the only ruined one in the Fylde) were photographed in 1949. Eyeing the dwindling stones with concern is Frank Walmsley, 'Mr. Garstang', who right up to his death was heart-and-soul interested in his native town and its preservation. He disliked the spread of bricks and mortar which destroyed character in the ancient market town, and particularly mourned 'the rape of Royal Oak Field', which had been the town's gathering-ground for decades. The castle, built in 1490 by the first Earl of Derby to protect lands which had once been held by King Richard III's supporters, was held for the king during the Civil War. It was the next to the last place to hold out against the forces of Parliament, and only the death of its governor led to a surrender. Although very strongly built, the battering it received then from cannon was aided down the years by pilfering of the massive stones.

St. Peter's Parish Church, Fleetwood, celebrated its centenary and patronal festival on 29th July 1941. The photograph shows the combined choirs from its Anglican churches. Dr J. M. Herbert, Bishop of Blackburn, preached at the commemoration service, referring to the 'hundredth milestone'. It was the first occasion in a hundred years of history that a priest had worn a festal cape during procession. In the congregation were the Mayor and Mayoress of Fleetwood (Alderman T. Clegg and Mrs Clegg), the Deputy Mayoress, town clerk, borough treasurer, sanitary inspector and other officials representing many sides of Fleetwood's life. Rejoicing at the centenary was restricted by the war, but a sense of pride and thankfulness in the spiritual welfare of a fishing village that had risen to Charter status was manifest. It found expression in the choirs' singing, accompanied by Mr E. Crompton, F.R.C.O., organist. The Vicar of Fleetwood at that time was the Revd S. G. Stanton.

Arranging the music for the pantomines was done by Miss Barbara Feather of Norbreck, one of the well-known characters of the Fylde affectionately remembered by generations of dancing girls. In 1949 she could look back on twenty-six years' experience of stage work. During the war Miss Feather, who studied music in London with a Dutchman who was one of Liszt's last pupils, was resident deputy organist for Blackpool Tower Company. In 1949 she was pianist for Charles Farrell, conductor of the Winter Gardens Band, and this indefatigable lady had at one time three bands in Cardiff. As solo accordianist, she gave several concerts in Blackpool and Sheffield. Among her memories in 1949 were the occasions on which she accompanied Paul Robeson, Phyllis Robins and Evelyn Laye. Miss Feather was married to Josef Herman, who took the part of Man Friday in Fleetwood's 1949 pantomine *Robinson Crusoe* (Chester Stage Academy's fourteenth annual pantomime).

Her interest, enthusiasm and zest for life communicated itself to the performers, as shown in this delightful group on the stage of the Lecture Hall at Thornton-Cleveleys (opened 19th November 1938). There was plenty of competition in the entertainment world. At Fleetwood's Marine Hall, 15th January 1949, Felix Mendelsohn and his Hawaian Serenaders invited 'Come and dance the hula hula to the music of the South Sea Islands — Admission *3s 6d, Forces 2s 6d.*'

'It is with great emotion that I forward these souvenirs . . . taken on that fateful day 1st June 1940 . . . thanks to the heroic crew of the *Gava* all my comrades were able to leave the hell of Dunkirk.' Thus wrote Alfred Dequinnemar from France on 7th November 1944, this photograph being one of his souvenirs.

On 27th May 1940 *Gava* sailed from Fleetwood in command of six trawlers, arriving at Dover on the 30th. Leaving Ramsgate for Dunkirk on 1st June, under attack by enemy aircraft, *Gava's* guns came into action and she was heavily bombarded, trying to get troops from the beaches and out of the sea. At 11.25 a.m. the French troops were embarked. At 11.40 there was renewed air attack. By 12.24 p.m. they left Dunkirk and cleared the harbour, *Gava* low in the water and laoded to the gunwales with her human cargo. A further three wounded French sailors were rescued when three of the *Gava's* crew dived overboard: Arthur Dunne, wireless operator, and deck-hands Harry Gawne and John Jones, all of whom were later awarded the O.B.E. for their bravery. Around 2.00 p.m. *Gava* was again under concentrated air attack. A further 137 survivors of the French destroyer *Foudroyant* were rescued at 2.18 with great difficulty, but by 9.00 p.m. all survivors and troops were ashore in Ramsgate.

The party on board *Gava* the night she docked at Ramsgate after nobly assisting at Dunkirk included a classic concoction by the cook — ten bottles of different wines and spirits from France mixed with 2 lb of sugar and a dozen eggs.

Street parties like this one in Blackpool after the surrender of the Japanese (V.J. Day) could not rise to such sumptuousness because of the scarcity of food and its strict rationing. Parties of this sort, however, were held all over the Fylde, as everywhere else in Britain, to celebrate. Overhung with horror at the Hiroshima death toll, yet relieved that the Second Word War was to finish, families clubbed together to provide for the children. Perhaps what was known as 'under the counter' or 'black market' provisions found their way on to the tables. Trips to the Isle of Man and Ireland unofficially supplemented Fylde rations. Some people had not seen real butter and eggs for years, and a banana or orange was a rarity. Milkmen were raised to a status unknown before, but the Fylde, being largely rural with its many farms and smallholdings, fared much better than the cities because they were able to grow fruit and vegetables, rear cattle and poultry and catch fish from the Irish Sea.

The party was in Dale Street. Japan's surrender is typified by the effigy of Tojo; the newsboy selling the *Evening Gazette* was made hero of the moment.

Princess Juliana of the Netherlands arrives at Fleetwood in October 1944, to be welcomed at the Town Hall by the Mayor, Councillor T. Roberts, J.P. Although the visit was officially restricted to the Dutch community, crowds of townspeople were eager to see her. Dock Street was thronged with many servicemen mingling with civilians, and by the time the party reached Nederlandsche Club, news of her arrival brought 2,000 people surging into Lord Street. She visited Holland House Hostel for Dutch seamen, which she inspected, and at the docks went on board two Dutch trawlers. Thirty Dutch seamen and one Dutch woman, Miss Sorgl, interpreter for Bloomfields Ltd., shook hands with Juliana, and the Mayor was able to tell her he had recently attended a Dutch party in honour of Queen Wilhelmina's birthday.

When the Germans overran Europe, Dutch and Belgian families, many connected with the trawling industry, fled to the north-west of Britain, some settling in Fleetwood. Mr A. Van Beirs, linked with Armement Ostendais, worked as a manager on the docks, and until his death regularly visited Fleetwood with his wife, in gratitude for the Fylde coast haven in the dangerous, dark early years of the war.

The growth of Blackpool as a resort meant that access became limited, especially from north and east approaches. In Poulton, Argyle Road, which ran into Moorland Road over the railway, became a side road when work was completed on Garstang Road East and West. The railway bridge was demolished when the new one was built, a mere fifty yards from the old. Ribbon development took place along the road's length, spreading from the junction with Hardhorn Road in both directions. The photograph shows work on this important carriageway. Gwen Yates, with whose parents the site foreman lodged during the building of the bridge, was taken over in a wheelbarrow when the bridge was completed. Gwen was proud and delighted to be the first over 't'new bridge on t'new road.' The term Poulton New Road persisted through the thirties and into the forties until it became, more mundanely, A586. The 1949 official *Guide to Poulton-le-Fylde,* price one shilling, calls it Garstang New Road and reveals the fast growth of trees planted down the sides. The speed of the traffic was by then becoming a matter for concern, following a number of tragic accidents.

A page of show business personalities scarcely comes amiss from one of the greatest entertainment centres on earth, Blackpool, situated on the Fylde coast. Their name is legion, but here we have four. Wilfred Pickles *(top, centre)* is wearing his Lancashire Fusiliers forage cap. He entertained in Blackpool, and radio was brightened by his show 'Have a Go', with Mabel at the table, Barney Colehan ('Give her the money, Barney') and Violet Carson, who played the piano. The latter was destined for fame as Ena Sharples of Coronation Street, and resided in the Fylde until her death. Reginald Dixon, *(top, left)*, 'Mr. Blackpool', who also lives here, became familiar to thousands, playing the mighty Wurlitzer organ in the Tower Ballroom, where it was installed in 1935. Another nostalgic reminder of the thirties and forties is the picture of Henry Hall *(top, right)* supported by two pretty girls at Blackpool Ice Drome in 1938. Leader of the B.B.C. Dance Orchestra, his signature tune 'Here's to the Next Time' was hummed and whistled universally. The fourth photograph shows George Formby *(below left)* having a joke with wife Beryl and friends. The first Miss Great Britain contest was in 1942. George was asked to judge the Beauty Queens' finals. He was a member of the Home Guard in Poulton in the war years, living in Mains Lane, Singleton.

No book on the Fylde could be complete without a windmill, and there have been corn mills on the site in this photograph (by the River Broadfleet at Pilling) since Norman times. This mill, pictured in the 1940s, had been inactive since 1926, the last of its line. Grass and bushes began to grow out of the mill top when it fell into disuse. The first mill was built around 1232, and in 1764 there were two mills, but the one depicted was designed by Ralph Slater, a famous millwright, who erected it on the remains of the old water mill. In such a windy area the whirling sails spun successfully until 1886, when a steam engine was installed and the sails taken down. Their wood was used for gateposts, beams and furniture, and the mill never looked the same again. *Gone With the Wind*, the book which along with Tolstoy's *War and Peace* was read in air raid shelters more than any other during Second World War years, comes to mind as a title appropriate to the photograph. With the splendid, humming sails went the grandeur and mystery which the windmill's modern refurbishing cannot replace.

In the 1940s old Glebe Farm and Tithebarn, visible just before entering St. Michael's-on-Wyre, were buildings of much interest, as the farm still had its thatched roof under corrugated iron. The photograph shows the datestone above the door of the farm: H T E 1713, the H probably referring to Hornby, the well-known local name. Attached on the right was the tithebarn with its inscription H T E 1710. It is a pity they were demolished, for they were examples of Fylde architecture which had stood for over two hundred years. The vast peat bogs of Rawcliffe, Pilling and Stalmine were present in Saxon and Danish times when the first settlement was formed, and what makes St. Michael's unique in the Fylde is that the church was already an ancient landmark when men and women formed into a community around it. In Saxon times the church was made of wood, the first stone church being built in the early thirteenth century. Doubtless there were ecclesiastical connections with Glebe Farm, which makes it doubly sad that the farm and tithebarn had to go after the forties era.

What the late George Mould termed 'Lancashire's unknown river' can be seen in this beautiful late forties' photograph of rural Fylde. The swollen River Wyre in winter, not far from Churchtown, illustrates its capacity to flood fields and invade streets at places such as Garstang, St. Michael's and Great Eccleston. Winding its way through the Fylde from its source near Abbeystead in the Bleasdale Fells to where it meets the sea at Fleetwood, the river contributes to industry, sport and leisure. During the war years when many had to have 'holidays at home', sunny days could be spent boating, swimming, paddling, fishing or just basking on its banks. It is many a day since its pellucid waters contained smelt and salmon. In 1939-40 the General Chemicals Division of I.C.I. moved into Hillhouse factory to build plant to manufacture products vital to the war effort. The land round about was still being farmed, and one of the farmer's daughters became a member of the Plastics Division canteen staff. Pollution of the Wyre increased, becoming severe at Fleetwood. Where fishermen could once go up-river for a catch when it was too stormy out at sea, fish were poisoned by effluent. Samphire, once harvested and pickled as a local delicacy, was rendered unusable as food.

The great church of St. Helen, Churchtown, 'cathedral of the Fylde', photographed in 1939, is only thirteen miles from Blackpool, in such a quiet, beautiful backwater that people today, as in the thirties and forties, drive past without knowing what they are missing. It was there before William the Conqueror's men visited the Fylde to draw up the Domesday Survey. Oak beams given by King Henry IV from the royal forest of Myerscough, registers going back to 1567, a massive leaning pillar 500 years old, a 600-year-old stone effigy, the chantry given by the Brockholes of Claughton, the crumbling schoolhouse in the churchyard where lie the bones of Scots who fell by the wayside in the marches of the '15 and '45 Rebellions, prove how deeply St. Helen's is steeped in history.

There was a Lune-mouth coastal hamlet called Glasson before ever Glasson Dock, shown in the photograph, was built. Begun in 1783, the dock was completed in 1791, and it remains an unusually quaint place, with its maritime air suddenly springing from green fields. Two big dock basins with stone sides and wide quays open into the Lune. The photograph from the thirties shows lock gates linking these. The River Conder, the Victoria, the Caribou Inn, the sandstone Custom House and the whitewashed coastguard's cottage were viewed by visitors who came in those days. Glasson Dock, although it never became the busy shipping centre visualized by Lancaster merchants, was still a port worthwhile for certain trades. Shipbuilding and repair was the principal work, Messrs Nicholson & Sons (established 1840) handling buoys, rigging, winches, ventilators, hatch covers etc. in their graving dock, but the late forties, although still coping with ocean-going craft, were also looking to a marina for the week-enders 'messing about in boats'.

This photograph is a memento of electioneering in the Fylde. The group in front of the vintage autobus stands in the lee of the parish church at Garstang. It was 1930 when R. P. Burnett hoped to represent Lancaster. He is in the middle of the back row behind the hatless lady. On the left beside the lady in white is John Chance, Fylde man, farmer and ardent campaigner for 'Save the Children', a phrase which doubtless referred to the dangers of malnutrition during the Depression and its aftermath.

The Bispham village of 1936 shown in the photograph has entirely vanished, but it was at that time a charming, old-world place with snow-white pebble walls, seventeenth-century cottages capped with thatch, and an ancient smithy. The best known of all its cottages, one built in 1686 by the Tinkler family, was Ivy Cottage Tea Rooms, which was visited by thousands of people staying in the Fylde during the thirties and forties. A carved date panel (E.T. E.T. R.T. 1686), buttery, firehood, crucks and claywalls, were all features of interest to the historians, and when the cottage was demolished in 1958 it was a sad occasion.

Fears were early voiced that all trace of old Bispham would disappear, and this became a reality with the knocking down of the smithy which used to be the farm lads' rendezvous. Ploughshares and coulters were sharpened here ready for the next day's work. The blacksmith sweated amidst the clatter of horses coming and going. The wheelwright whittled away at wood, heating iron hoops to be burned on to the wooden-wheel rims, which were cooled and contracted by tossing them down a handy well. Mr William Singleton, one of the village's oldest residents, knew Smithy Cottage intimately, it being his parents' first home.

A float from the Carleton Gala in the thirties depicting Mary, quite contrary, with her pretty maids all in a row. The little girls have captured the spirit of both the day and the age with that touch of aspidistra plants, far left and right. The aspidistra, popular symbol of domestic respectability, had weathered Victorian and Edwardian ages, but by King George V's reign was 'going out', despised, along with bamboo tables and other bric-à-brac (now once again thought charming). Castle Gardens Hotel is in the background. It was every Carleton girl's dream to be crowned Rose Queen under the wrought-iron archway which originally had sported a castellated entrance to the Pleasure Gardens, giving the inn its name. Following the crowning ceremony by a local 'bigwig' or gracious lady, the procession moved off to Pye's farm with Morris dancers and bands whilst the Queen, in glorious velvet cape and flowered crown, rode in a landau with her retinue.

Marton Moss was the home of the glasshouse industry in the Fylde, producing tomatoes, lettuce, cucumbers, chrysanthemums. In the thirties and forties the industry spread to other parts — Warton, Freckleton, Great Ecleston, Elswick and Newton-with-Clifton. Good summers saw poor prices because of a glut in the market, but in 1931 Albert William Plummer of Harbour Lane, Warton, revolutionized lettuce growing by planting his glasshouse with lettuce in September, after his tomato crop, to send them for sale in Manchester by November. Before this, only French lettuce had been available. Despite Fylde farming comments of 'Dig 'em in lad, you'll never sell 'em,' sell they did at *3s 6d* per dozen. Spring lettuce were bringing only *1s 6d* per dozen, so Albert soon had followers. He also pioneered French beans under glass, a practice which he continued until war broke out in 1939. After the war many of the older glasshouses were in urgent need of repair and, faced with colossal charges, growers went out of business, tempted to sell their land for building. Gone are the days when you could drive through the Moss and see nurseries adjacent to each other, a thriving glasshouse industry where people took pleasure in picking tomatoes by the hundred and packing boxes of lettuce or chrysanthemums for East Lancashire, Yorkshire, Brimingham and Newcastle. Albert Plummer's fine lettuces and vintage glasshouses were photographed on 4th December 1935.

Helping with the War Effort made 1942 yet another eventful and busy year in the Fylde. The iron railings from the Mount were sawn off and piled on to the growing mountain of scrap metal. Chief Petty Officer John Hearty went to Buckingham Palace to receive the D.S.O. from King George VI 'for conspicuous work carried out under dangerous conditions'. Fleetwood's Warship Week began on 6th March, with its aim to adopt H.M.S. *Turbulent*. 'Hit Back with War Savings' was the slogan. Thornton reached the target for Warship Week — £120,000, towards a corvette. Garstang sent £150,000 to adopt H.M.S. *Bleasdale*. By June the ladies' fire-fighting team was at full strength, all set to extinguish incendiary bombs. A National Waste Paper Contest in January 1942 enabled towns to compete for a prize of £500. *Pepperpot Penelope,* Blackpool's adopted ship, earned her nickname in Malta, where she was continually under fire during her two weeks' stay, and a Fylde girl, Mary Squires, expert net braider and canvas sewer, made a hammock in two hours for an injured airman who needed it. At that time, Burton's, men's outfitters, was able to produce a regulation officer's greatcoat, naval, R.A.F. or military style, for *135s*.

Great Eccleston, appearing untouched by events, had not yet parted with her cast-iron railings. Only in 1932 did electricity come to the village, the first connection being on 18th December; the Women's Institute was formed in January 1931. Two main events dominated the year, Gala Day and the Great Eccleston Agricultural Show, which had been formed by joining three ancient cattle fairs.

In this photograph is the Lancashire lass who became the most highly paid entertainer in the world, 'Our Gracie', generous benefactress to the Fylde coast in her provision of convalescent homes for children. She performed many times in Blackpool and took that town by storm, making the hit film of the 1930s' *Sing as We Go*. Although the Lancashire seaside towns and their inhabitants were the butt of many of her jokes, she had a genuine affection, which was fully reciprocated, for them.

On the far left of the photograph, next to Mrs Saer, is the Mayor, Captain Charles C. Saer, a well-known Fylde man who devoted forty-three years' service to education. From the Testimonial School at Fleetwood he became headmaster at Milton Street; in his first year at Fleetwood he received an annual salary of £75, but as school monitor in 1885 he received only one shilling a week. When a detachment of the King's Own Lancasters was formed he was a volunteer. In his lengthy, distinguished service Charles Saer helped to raise £100,000 during the 1927 Great Flood, and, to cap his popularity, was also a prominent footballer who played in twenty league games. When the foreshore improvements were going forward in the thirties, he opened the new outdoor pool with a gold key and swam a length of the baths. In June 1933 Charles Saer retired from teaching, but continued to busy himself in Fleetwood affairs.

Linking arms with Gracie Fields on the right is Tom Roberts, J.P., who was Mayor in 1942. This occasion, where Gracie Fields is the guest of honour, is a dinner at the Marine Hall, Fleetwood.

West View, a double-fronted detached house standing next to Ball's garage at the corner of Fleetwood Road and Hatfield Road. This striking building could still be seen by passers-by in the 1940s. It eventually came down to make way for extensions to the petrol-filling station in 1964. Built in 1881 for Mr Berry, a master brickmaker, it was sited on the highest ground in the area, because of vulnerability to floods. An additional protective mound was constructed, and on more than one occasion it has been completely surrounded by the sea. Mr Berry had his brick croft on adjoining land, and traces of the kilns could still be seen in the thirties and forties. The clay for hand-made bricks came from fields and large hollows in the Fylde. Many houses in the area were built from Berry's bricks. The grain elevator on Wyre Dock used them, and when it was demolished in the late forties, bricks from there 'came home', going into extensions to Ball's garage. Mr Jack Calderbank, a marine engineer who played cricket for Fleetwood, lived at West View after Mr Duckworth, who had followed Mr Berry. The Ball family took over ownership of the house in 1926, but in early days it was a lonely spot, its nearest neighbour being Flakefleet Farm. The name of the house gave this area on the outskirts of Fleetwood its name.

In 1948 only one and three quarter hours of television was transmitted in the evenings, so wireless was popular. It was a heat-wave year and the New Look was launched: long, voluminous skirts, ridiculed by many, but an obvious reaction to no material, no style and the purchase of clothes limited by coupons. Even the men became more daring in hat styles, but shortages continued: queues for cigarettes, as there had been for No. 8 torch batteries eight years before in the blackout days of war.

In spite of world upheaval, some old crafts died hard. In the fine photograph from the late forties, Austin Walmsley and his son Austin are shaping the point of a road-mending implement called a 'scarifier tyne'. The two men are making the sparks fly on the anvil, almost half a century old then. The Walmsley business, founded in 1902 by Bruno Walmsley and his five sons, entailed working on the old forge, but although much trade dwindled with less horse power, this is one craft that has escaped the march of time in Garstang. When the photograph was taken there were still five horses from local farms that needed regular shoeing, and the firm is still in business to this day, although operating from Green Lane West industrial estate.